Published in 2022 by Orange Mosquito
An Imprint of Welbeck Children's Limited
part of Welbeck Publishing Group.

Based in London and Sydney.

www.welbeckpublishing.com

Design and layout © Mosquito Books Barcelona, SL 2022
Text © Soledad Romero Mariño 2022
Illustration © María Beorlegi 2022
Translated by Howard Curtis
Publisher: Margaux Durigon
Production: Clare Hennessy

For Luciano. My eyes and my heart in these mountains.
SOLEDAD

ISBN: 9781914519284
eISBN: 9781914519291

Printed in Spain

10 9 8 7 6 5 4 3 2 1

Soledad Romero Mariño and María Beorlegi

HIMALAYA

The wonders of the mountains that touch the sky

ORANGE

M·O·S·Q·U·I·T·O

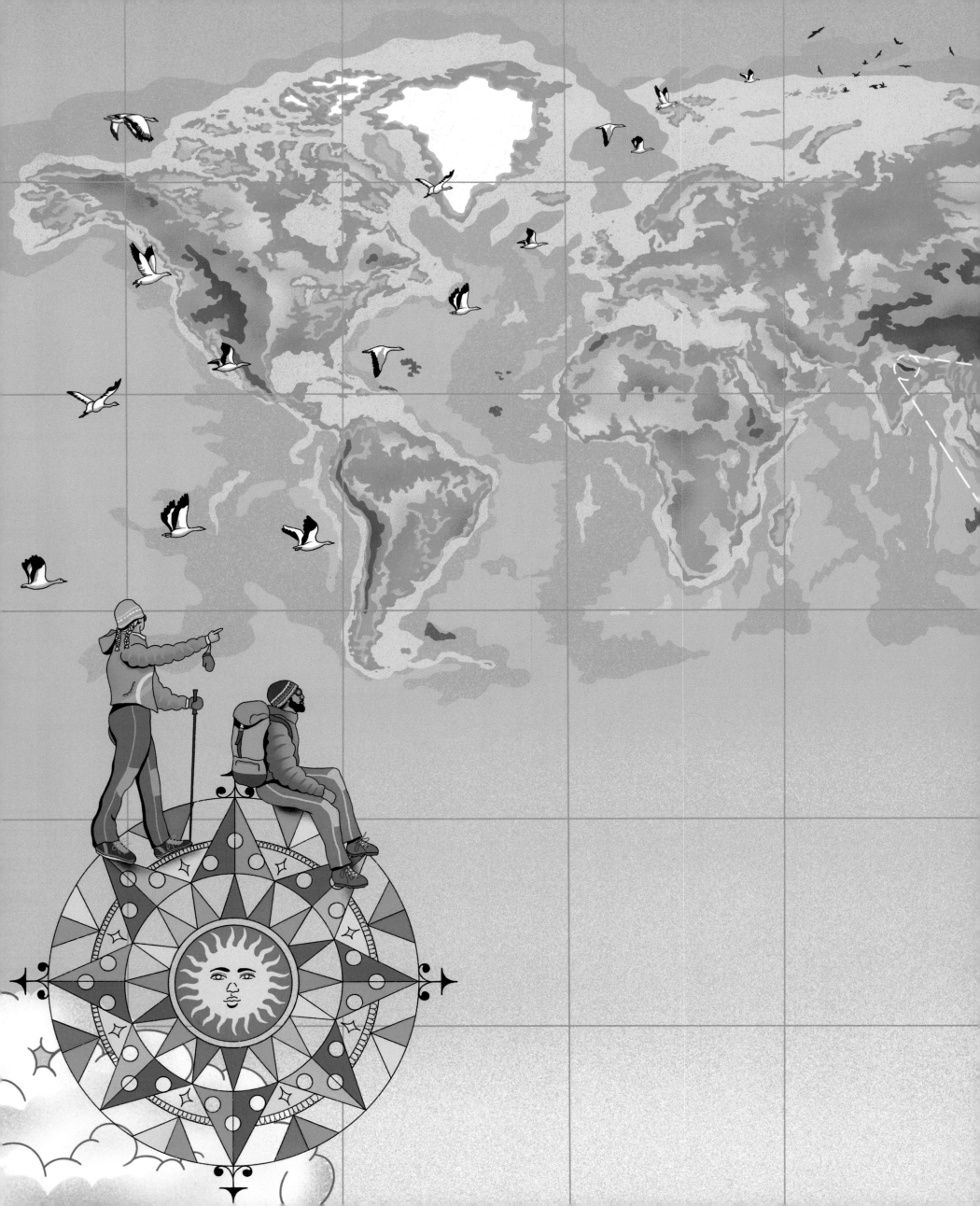

THE HIMALAYAS
THE ABODE OF SNOW

Himalayas, from the Sanskrit *jimālaia*, jima (snow)
and *alaia* (abode): 'Abode of snow'

The spectacular mountain range of the Himalayas was formed 50 million
years ago. Planet Earth was living through its tertiary era, which came after
the big dinosaurs went extinct. The tumultuous movement of plates in
this time created new continents, oceans, and mountain ranges.

It was a massive collision between what we now know as India and Asia
that led to the formation of the highest mountainous region in the world.
The collision of these land masses forced the Earth's crust up; and the awesome
Himalayas rose above the earth. 14 of its summits climbed to over 26,000 feet.
In a monumental effort to reach the stars, these mountains became the highest
and—what many consider to be—the most beautiful peaks on the planet.

This book follows the magnificent Himalayan range through the lands of Nepal,
India and Tibet. The Himalayas are not only the summit of the world, they are also
home to millions of people who live closest to the natural soul of our planet.

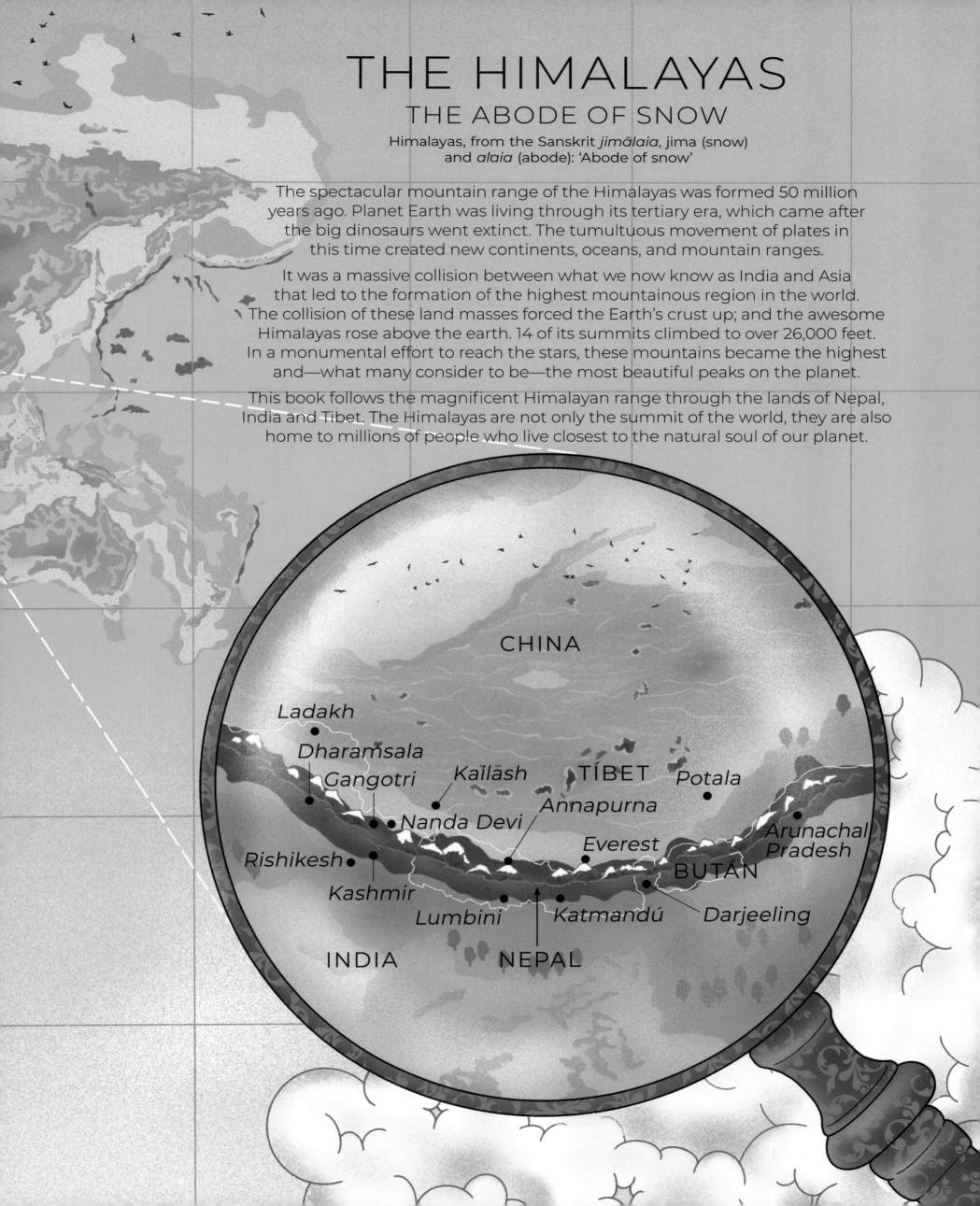

THE HEART OF THE HIMALAYAS

NEPAL

Nepal, from the Tibetan *niyampal*: 'sacred land'

Nepal is a landlocked country nestled in the heart of the Himalayas. For centuries it has been a valued gateway between India and China. The constant movement of traders, pilgrims, and travelers crossing Nepal from one side of the Himalayas to the other has marked its lively history.

Recent excavations in the southern part of Nepal have revealed the remains of people dating as far back as the Neolithic period (12,000 years ago). However, it wasn't until the Middle Ages—around the fifteenth century—that Nepal became a country of magnificent temples and a golden gateway between the giant Asian countries of India and China.

The colorful prayer flags of Nepal—found throughout the Himalayan region—represent the wishes of the people and offer protection for the place where they live. Their colors symbolize the five elements of Buddhism: blue for the sky; white for water; red for fire; green for air; and yellow for the Earth.

Nepal is the only country in the world with a non-rectangular flag. Its two triangles represent the mountains of the Himalayas, and also the two religions that live side-by-side in the country: Hinduism and Buddhism.

TREKKING OFFICE & SNOOKER

The Himalayan Skin Art

TATTOO

SERVICE CENTER

THE CAPITAL OF NEPAL
KATHMANDU

Kathmandu, from the Tibetan *Kasthamandap*: a wooden structure on the Durbar Square.

The heart of this medieval city is Durbar Square—listed as a UNESCO World Heritage site. Thousands of people gather here every day to admire the beauty of Kathmandu's gorgeous temples and stunning, hand-carved statues of the gods. Before the unification of Nepal, this dynamic country was divided into individual kingdoms. In a demonstration of power and individuality, each kingdom had its own Durbar Square (which means Royal Square) built in front of their royal palaces. These ancient squares hold the living memory of the people's legends and beliefs.

←First Floor←

LAUNDRY Rs. 50/- Per Kg INSIDE

Kathmandu is both the capital and the largest city in Nepal. It is a magnificent, riotous mix of noise, bicycles, rickshaws, peddlers' stalls, freely roaming cows, statues, monkeys, thousand-year-old palaces, mountaineers, and travelers.

LOYAL CARGO DHL

NEPA Institute

Three million people live in this extraordinary city that has risen up in the valley that bears its name.

During religious festivals, the squares become large stages hosting mass gatherings, magnificent offerings, music, and dancing that pay tribute to the gods.

BHAKTAPUR

One of three ancient kingdoms that fought for control of the Kathmandu Valley; this city is considered to be the loveliest and is distinguished by picturesque alleys, temples, pagodas*, and gorgeous squares.

ANCIENT CITIES
THE KATHMANDU VALLEY

Without losing their essential spirit, the cities of the Kathmandu Valley have been able to absorb everything that visitors have brought to these lands over the centuries.

PATAN

A city full of ornate palaces, enchanting courtyards, and mysterious temples, with the distinction of having the most spectacular Durbar Square in the valley. It is also a market city, where Nepal's finest produce can be found.

* Pagoda: a building on several levels, typical of the Hindu religion. They are pretty, rustic structures of brick and wood, with roofs of clay.

** Pinnacle: Cone-shaped feature situated in the highest part of a building.

SWAYAMBHUNATH

This religious site is located on top of a hill in the highest part of the Valley. At the top of 365 steps stands the most sacred stupa (domed Buddhist shrine) in Nepal. The eyes of Buddha are depicted on its golden pinnacle**. From that height, the eyes see everything that happens in the valley and beyond.

ROUTES

There are two main routes to the top
of Everest:

FROM THE SOUTH-EAST:

This route, which starts in Nepal, presents no climbing
challenges, but climbers must still face the inevitable
altitude sickness, bad weather, wind, avalanches, and
must cross dangerous and unpredictable expanses
of ice (such as the Khumbu Icefall).

FROM THE NORTH:

This route, which starts in Tibet, is more difficult technically and is
exclusively for experienced climbers. Before beginning the great expedition,
Sherpas teach the climbers about their spiritual beliefs. While still at
Base Camp, the Sherpas perform a ceremony, asking the mountain for
permission to climb it.

EVEREST BASE CAMP
5364m

THE TOP OF THE WORLD
EVEREST

Everest is named after Sir George Everest, one of the first British surveyors to investigate the range. In Nepal, the mountain is known as Sagarmāthā: "Head in the sky." In Tibet, it is called Chomolungma or Qomolangma: "Mother of the universe."

Located on the border between Nepal and Tibet, Everest is the highest summit on the planet, rising to 29,031 feet. No place on Earth is closer to the sky and its storms are treacherous; reaching its peak is the special privilege of the bravest and luckiest climbers. Those who reach the summit of Everest can only spend a few minutes on "top of the world." The descent has to be undertaken before night falls or before the oxygen the climbers have brought with them (in bottles) runs out.

SHERPAS

Sherpas are an ethnic group who inhabit this mountain area. It is also the name given to the skilled local guides who have adapted to the mountain region's high altitudes. They are the toughest, strongest, and bravest people up here. Their abilities are essential: without them as guides and helpers, nobody would be able to reach any of the summits in the Himalayas, let alone the dreamed-of summit of Everest.

To the South, the legendary Pokhara Valley offers the best views of the whole Himalayan range.

EVEREST'S BEAUTIFUL SISTER
ANNAPURNA

Annapurna, from the Sanskrit: "goddess of the harvests" or "goddess of abundance"

Annapurna is a mountainous massif situated at the heart of the Himalayas. Of all its mountains, Annapurna I is the highest. At a height of 26,547 feet, this peak is number 10 out of the 14 highest mountains in the whole world. The massif is 34 miles of majestic connected mountains surrounded by extraordinary beauty. Its lands are protected and form the largest park in all of Nepal.

Annapurna is a remote mountain area. The inhabitants live as they did in the past: they cultivate the land and raise animals; they load baggage on their backs and transport it slowly along paths built in past centuries.

At the foot of the massif is the astonishing gorge of Kali Gandaki, believed to be the deepest in the world. In one of the most extraordinary journeys across the magnificent range, hikers from all over the world walk the steep paths and cross the fascinating hanging bridges. On the Northeast face, the wild crystalline waters of the River Marshyangdi tumble down from the frozen massif.

THE CRADLE OF BUDDHA
LUMBINI

Buddha, from the Sanskrit: "the Awakened One" or "the Enlightened One."

Buddha was born in the temple of Maya Devi in Lumbini, a town in Nepal near the border with India. Before becoming Buddha, he was Prince Siddhartha Gautama.

The story begins 2,500 years ago. The young prince Siddhartha lived surrounded by luxury and isolated from any kind of misery.

He began to live as an ascetic (a holy man), without possessions and without pleasures—and practically without food. Siddhartha only meditated in the deepest silence. Weak and almost dead from hunger, Siddhartha realized that he had to find a middle way between luxury and poverty. Only then would he have the lucidity and strength to find spiritual answers.

But one day, beyond the walls of his temple, he saw an old man, a sick man, a dead person, and an ascetic (a holy man). Moved by the suffering that had been hidden from him throughout his life, young Siddhartha abandoned his luxurious home and set out on a solitary journey in search of answers.

It was then, after meditating for weeks in the shade of a fig tree, that Siddhartha reached the great "enlightenment." Darkness turned to light, and Siddhartha became Buddha.

As Buddha, he devoted his life to sharing what he had learned while traveling through the north of India. This was the birth of Buddhism.

For centuries, Buddhists have traveled to the sacred places visited by the master. In these places we also find monks intoning mantras who have dedicated their lives to Buddhism; we recognize them by their shaven heads and red robes.

MULTICOLORED HIMALAYAS

INDIA

It is the red of the sandstone used to build its palaces. It is the blue, white, red, green, and yellow of the prayer flags flapping in the wind. It is the purple and pink of the millions of flowers that grow by the lakes and in the valleys. It is the bright colors worn by the women. It is the golden sunset. And it is also the silvery dusk over the dreamlike Himalayas.

When the magnificent Himalayan range enters India, a wonderful multicolored fan opens up. The cultural diversity, the temples, and the spectacular landscapes add color to the white summits of the mountains.

Hinduism is the main religion practiced here, by people who have lived side by side in India for centuries. Considered to be the world's oldest religion, Hinduism is a wondrous, colorful mixture of beliefs and philosophies without a central spiritual figure.

THE REFUGE OF
THE DALAI LAMA
DHARAMSALA

Dharamshala, from the Hindi: refuge or
place of rest for spiritual pilgrims.

According to legend, the Dalai Lama is the reincarnation of Buddha on Earth. After his death, his soul returns to Earth in the body of a new-born baby—and so on, forever. In 1959, the 14th Dalai Lama was living in peace in Tibet, a small and delightful country in the north of the Himalayas. But due to political conflict, he and his followers had to abandon Tibet in a hurry. The Prime Minister of India opened his borders and offered the Tibetans a place to live. The location was a beautiful area called McLeod Ganj, in the high part of the city of Dharamshala.

MCLEOD GANJ

This suburb stands on high rocks to the west of the Himalayas. Here, the Dalai Lama and his followers found peace and a new home very similar to their longed-for Tibet. That is why McLeod Ganj is also known affectionately as "Little Lhasa" (Lhasa is the capital of Tibet, where the Dalai Lama used to live). In McLeod Ganj, everything revolves around spiritual exercise. At dawn, the murmur of mantras drift across the mountains. And during the rest of the day, the monks meditate, chant, or walk in silence in their distinctive red robes. It is a place reserved for Tibetan Buddhism and a living reflection of the unreachable Tibet, which lives on eternally in the hearts of its inhabitants.

THE CRADLE OF YOGA
RISHIKESH

Rishikesh, from the Sanskrit: 'Lord of the Senses'

Rishikesh is a sacred city situated at the foot of the Himalayas and is therefore known as the gateway to the Himalayas. In this place, the River Ganges makes its magnificent entry into the territory of India. The Hindus chose this area of the river to build their legendary ashrams: houses where pupils and masterś engage in spiritual practices such as meditation and yoga. Meditation is a series of exercises to train the mind, to be in the present moment and reach the deepest part of the self. They may be exercises in breathing, concentration, or visualization. Ideally, the exercises are done sitting down, with the spine straight, and in a quiet place. Yoga (from the Sanskrit for "union") is the discipline that unites the exercises of meditation with physical exercises or postures called asanas. This practice combines mental and physical work.

Both meditation and yoga are beneficial for all types of people: healthy or sick, women and men, children and grown-ups. They are thousand-year-old disciplines, part of the eternal quest for well-being.

KANCHENJUNGA

This is the third highest mountain in the world at 28,169 feet and the sturdiest of the Himalayas' highest peaks. At dawn, the reflection of the sun's rays on the white summit lights up the slope where Darjeeling, a small city dedicated to the growing of tea, is situated.

In Darjeeling, the slope is entirely covered by green plantations. And the pickers, with hundreds of years of tradition in their hands, carefully detach the tender shoots from the shrub. The first crop of the year, in mid-March, is the most delicious.

DELIGHTFUL TEA PLANTATIONS

DARJEELING

Darjeeling, from the Tibetan *dorje* (rayo) and *ling* (place): 'The land of the ray'

During the years of British rule, Darjeeling was chosen as a summer holiday destination because of its pleasant climate. With the massive influx of the British, it grew in size. They built bungalows and a steam railway, and its unforgettable tea began a journey around the world. Darjeeling leapt to fame as the city of tea, an emerald-green city in the Himalayas.

The tea plantations are as sacred as they are beautiful, which is why they are thought of as gardens, not as farms. In addition, the exquisite taste and fragrance of the black tea is recognized as the crème de la crème of tea throughout the world.

Darjeeling's black tea is a delicate drink with a soft color, a floral aroma, and a sweet, refreshing taste.

LITTLE TIBET
LADAKH

Ladakh, from the Hindi: 'land of high passes'

Ladakh is a sacred place between the Kunlun Mountains in the north and the Himalayas in the south. It is also known as Little Tibet. When the Dalai Lama lived in Tibet, Ladakh was part of his empire. Its people have remained quite isolated in the high mountains, keeping alive the traditions of Tibetan Buddhism.

Ladakh is situated on a cold, windy plateau. Only the waters of the River Indus cross the steppe. Colored prayer flags flutter resolutely and chants rise above the roofs of the Tibetan monasteries, drifting across the desert beneath the vigilant gaze of the all-powerful Himalayas.

THE VALLEY OF THE FLOWERS

NANDA DEVI

Nanda Devi, from the Hindi: 'Goddess who brings happiness'

The Nanda Devi Valley (Valley of the Flowers) circles around the Nanda Devi, the second highest mountain in India. Spectacularly protected by nature, the summit and its surroundings are almost inaccessible. A formidable crown of twelve peaks more than 21,000 feet high shelters this lovely area, also known as the Nanda Devi Sanctuary. The Valley of the Flowers is a gorgeous floral paradise, both a National Park and a UNESCO World Heritage site.

The mountains rise up on the horizon. And fantastic animals, such as multicolored butterflies and red foxes, fly and run freely over the verdant glades.

The Valley of the Flowers is also home to valuable medicinal plants. It is a world of delightful sensations and fragrances. Another gift it offers is the most colorful summit in the Himalayas at sunset.

At a height of 11,810 feet the beauty of the Valley is unequaled. Transparent streams irrigate the earth while millions of orchids, marigolds, daisies, and poppies carpet the slope with bright colors.

MAHARAJAS' PARADISE
THE KASHMIR VALLEY

The name of the valley derives from the process of drought that created it.
Ka (water) *Shimir* (to drain): 'a land drained of water'.

Situated in the westernmost part of the Indian Himalayas, the Kashmir Valley has for centuries been a paradisiacal home to maharajas and emperors. It is a place of great beauty and great wealth. In the Kashmir Valley, everything revolves around its great fertile Lake Dal.

MARKETS

The markets are also built on the lake. Many buyers and sellers trade fruit, vegetables, and flowers from boats.

SRINAGAR

This is the capital of Kashmir, built on the shores of the lake. Here we find the most beautiful wooden houses in India, and its bazaars sell highly prized cashmere wool handicrafts.

CASHMERE WOOL

This is the wool of the cashmere goat, an animal that originated in the mountains of Tibet. It is a rare and very special wool, extremely soft, silky, and light to the touch. It is a luxury product for fighting the cold, which makes it a symbol of style and elegance famous throughout the world.

SHIKARAS

On the lake, everything floats over its calm waters. Men and women move about in shikaras, the lake's traditional dugout canoes.

THE SNOW LEOPARD
ARUNACHAL PRADESH

Arunachal Pradesh, from the Hindi: 'land of the rising sun'

Arunachal Pradesh is the Indian state situated at the easternmost end of the range.
From its horizon the first rays of the sun reach the Himalayas.

More than a hundred tribal groups live on the slopes of Arunachal Pradesh. They are very religious, with almost half the population being faithful to Dony-Polo. This is an animistic religion which believes that everything has a soul, including rivers, trees, and mountains.

DID YOU KNOW?

This extraordinary inhabitant of Arunachal Pradesh lives alone
in the mountains and there are many legends about it.

The snow leopard has soft, thick, gray, almost white fur and a long,
bushy tail in which it wraps itself to shelter from the cold. This animal is
a fierce predator, capable of hunting prey three times larger than itself.

Among cats, its leap is one of the longest and most powerful.

It hunts by day, walking with quiet ease on the
snow, thanks to its padded paws.

The snow leopard is the only leopard that doesn't roar. Its throat
could manage a roar, so it is a mystery why it doesn't.

Its gestation period is just over three months. The female
normally gives birth to two cubs, but up to five are possible.
By the age of two, the cubs are considered adults.

The snow leopard is another of the world's magnificent animals
that are in danger of extinction. It is estimated that barely 5,000
of them run free on the white summits of the Himalayas.

THE SOURCE OF THE GANGES
GANGOTRI

Running from the Gangotri glacier is the River Bhagirathi, the main source of the Ganges and the spiritual home to the goddess Maa Ganga (the mother of the Ganges). The Bhagirathi is the most powerful source of water in India and one of the most sacred Hindu pilgrimage sites.

Bhagirathi in Sanskrit means "caused by Bhagiratha". Bhagiratha was a prince who, according to legend, asked the goddess Maa Ganga to free his ancestors from a curse. She came down from the sky in the form of the River Ganges, with purifying powers in her waters—this is why Hindus bathe in the Ganges: to cleanse their souls. In addition, they throw the ashes of the dead in the river to avoid reincarnation. They believe that the deceased should not have to return to Earth and begin a new life.

At the beginning of the 18th century, the Nepalese general Amar Singh Thapa built a temple dedicated to the goddess Maa Ganga, combining the power of legend and the beauty of the Himalayas.

THE SOUL OF THE HIMALAYAS
TIBET

Tibet rises to a height of 16,075 feet on a large plateau beyond the Himalayas. It is the highest region in the world and for 300 years was the peaceful home of the Dalai Lamas. Gradually the Buddhism practiced in this region began to be known as Lamaism or Tibetan Buddhism.

Tibetan Buddhism is a great inspiration not only to the people of the Himalayas, but also to others around the world. Its practices and teachings help people of all countries and all races, who find in the words of Buddha a path to spiritual peace or, to put it another way, a path to happiness.

Its messages are based on peace, love, and respect for everything that exists in the Universe.

"If you truly loved yourself, you could never hurt another."

Buddha

THE HOME OF THE DALAI LAMA

POTALA

Potala: from the Sanskrit "Land where the Buddha of compassion lives"

Lhasa is the capital of Tibet and on its hill stands Potala Palace. Most Tibetan buildings are elevated and are generally built of stone, wood, and earth. There is no better example of Tibetan architecture than the stunning Potala Palace.

Potala Palace began as a modest place devoted to meditation but grew until it became the thirteen-storey Red Palace and White Palace we see today. It is a magnificent masterpiece, built by 7,000 laborers and 1,500 artisans over a period of more than 15 years.

Nowadays, Potala Palace is a museum and its rightful owner—the Dalai Lama—lives in exile in India. Thousands of pilgrims visit to walk around it in a circle, praying and mourning the loss of these sacred lands.

THE RED PALACE

This central building is the most sacred part of the structure, dedicated exclusively to prayer. It is a labyrinth of 13 storeys with many halls, chapels, and shrines. Everything is decorated with gorgeous engravings, paintings and works of art bestowed by emperors of ancient dynasties. It is in the Red Palace that the richest stupas are found, beneath brilliant golden towers.

THE WHITE PALACE

This building surrounds the Red Palace and is spread over two wings. These areas were designed to accommodate the princes and the Dalai Lamas. It is in this part of the Palace that day to day political and social activities are carried out. The White Palace has the East Hall and the Hall of the Sun as well as offices and bedrooms. This part of the Palace is also meticulously decorated with gorgeous murals, frescos, and paintings that depict the history and legends of this thousand-year-old land.

NOMADIC PEOPLE
TIBETAN ETHNIC GROUPS

The Tibetan people consist of numerous ethnic groups. Loyal to their own traditions, they live peacefully on this cold, high plateau. Most are herders who wander the steppes in search of pasture for their herds, in rhythm with nature and the seasons.

THE YAK
(*Bos mutus* or *Bos grunniens*)

This is a bovine mammal with long, fleecy black fur.
They live on the high, cold mountains of Asia and the Himalayas.
They can live in the wild, but most have been domesticated.
The males can reach up to 6.5 feet in height and weigh
up to 2,200 pounds.

Traditional dress is commonly worn by Tibetans.
You'll often notice that men wear their hair long
and tied with a ribbon, high on their heads; women
tend to wear plaits. Most locals wear leather boots
and clothes that protect from the cold: trousers
for the men and long skirts for the women.

THE MOST SACRED PEAK IN ASIA
KAILASH

Kailash from the Sanskrit: 'crystal'

In Tibetan it is called *Gang Rinpoche*: 'precious jewel of the snows'.

Kailash is another of the spectacular peaks in the Himalayan range. The mountain rises strong and resplendent between Lake Manasarovar and Rakshastal. Four rivers flow from its summit across Asia; they are the rivers Sutlej, Karnali, Brahmaputra and Indus.

Many religions believe this mountain is Paradise, the final destination of the soul. According to Hindu texts, the god Shiva lives at the top of Kailash and its four slopes are made of precious materials (crystal, ruby, gold, and lapis lazuli).

It is forbidden for people to climb the Kailash summit—only the soul that reaches Paradise can ascend to its white summit. Thousands of pilgrims come to Kailash to walk in a sacred circle around the mountain peak. The energy of the place is overwhelming, and the walkers feel the presence of the gods during their exhausting walk. According to pilgrims, when they have walked all the way around the mountain, their soul is assured entry into Paradise.

Kailash is also considered the center of the world. Its massif rises like a pillar to the sky. The beauty of Kailash is deeply moving, and its powerful energy emerges brightly above the mountains of the Himalayas.